D1691028

First published in Great Britain in 1990 by
COLLINS & BROWN LIMITED
Mercury House
195 Knightsbridge
London SW7 1RE

Copyright © Collins & Brown 1990
Illustrations copyright © Ditz 1990

The right of Ditz to be identified as the creator of the illustrations in this work has been asserted by her in accordance with the Copyright, Designs and Patents Act 1988 and she further asserts the artist's right of integrity and of paternity in the illustrations.

All rights reserved. No part of this publication may be reproduced, stored in a retrieval system, or transmitted in any form or by any means electronic, mechanical, photocopying, recording or otherwise, without the prior written permission of the copyright owner.

A CIP catalogue record for this book is available from the British Library

ISBN 1 85585 095 8

Conceived, edited and designed by Collins & Brown

EDITOR
Gabrielle Townsend
RESEARCHED BY
Sarah Bloxham
Samantha Martyr
ART DIRECTOR
Roger Bristow
DESIGNED BY
Mathewson Bull

Reproduction by Mandarin Offset, Hong Kong
Printed and bound in Hong Kong by Mandarin Offset

EVERLASTING
Diary

ILLUSTRATED WITH PAINTINGS BY
DITZ

C&B
Collins & Brown

January

THE SNOW CATS

January

1

2

There had been just enough snow to cover the earth and all its covers with one sheet of pure and uniform white, and just time enough since the snow had fallen to allow the hedges to be freed of their fleecy load, and clothed with a delicate coating of rime. The atmosphere was deliciously calm; soft, even mild, in spite of the thermometer; no perceptible air, but a stillness that might almost be felt, the sky, rather gray than blue, throwing out in bold relief the snow-covered roofs of our village, and the rimy trees that rise above them, and the sun shining dimly as through a veil, giving a pale fair light, like the moon, only brighter. There was a silence, too, that might become the moon, as we stood at our little gate looking up the quiet street; a Sabbath-like pause of work and play, rare on a work-day.

MARY RUSSELL MITFORD

January

3

5

4

6

January

THE OLD YEAR'S *gone away*
  To nothingness and night:
We cannot find him all the day
  Nor hear him in the night:
He left no footstep, mark or place
  In either shade or sun:
The last year he'd a neighbour's face,
  In this he's known by none.

JOHN CLARE

7

8

9

January

10

11

12

When silver snow decks Sylvio's clothes
   And jewel hangs at shepherd's nose,
We can abide life's pelting storm
That makes our limbs quake, if our hearts
   be warm.

Whilst Virtue is our walking-staff
And Truth a lantern to our path,
We can abide life's pelting storm
That makes our limbs quake, if our hearts
   be warm.

Blow, boisterous wind, stern winter frown,
Innocence is a winter's gown;
So clad, we'll abide life's pelting storm
That makes our limbs quake, if our hearts
   be warm.

WILLIAM BLAKE

January

13

14

15

16

January

17

18

19

20

January

W<small>HEN ICICLES HANG</small> *by the wall,*
  And Dick the shepherd blows his nail,
And Tom bears logs into the hall,
  And milk comes frozen home in pail;
When blood is nipped, and ways be foul,
Then nightly sings the staring owl.
Tu-whit, to-who! a merry note,
While greasy Joan doth keel the pot.

WILLIAM SHAKESPEARE

21

22

23

January

24

26

25

27

January

28

29

30

31

February

THE BLUE TIT WINDOW

February

1

2

3

The masterful wind was up and out, shouting and chasing, the lord of the morning. Poplars swayed and tossed with a roaring swish; dead leaves sprang aloft, and whirled into space; and all the clear-swept heaven seemed to thrill with sound like a great harp. It was one of the first awakenings of the year. The earth stretched herself, smiling in her sleep; and everything leapt and pulsed to the stir of the giant's movement.

KENNETH GRAHAME

February

4

5

6

7

February

8

9

A DEEP SNOW UPON *the ground... The sun shone bright and clear.* A deep stillness in the thickest part of the wood, undisturbed except by the occasional dropping of the snow from the holly boughs; no other sound but that of the water, and the slender notes of a redbreast, which sang at intervals on the outskirts of the southern side of the wood. The whole appearance of the wood was enchanting; and each tree taken singly, was beautiful. The branches of the hollies pendent with their white burden, but still showing their bright red berries, and their glossy green leaves. The bare branches of the oak thickened by snow.

DOROTHY WORDSWORTH

February

10

11

12

13

February

14

15

16

*The red-breast, sacred to the household
   gods,*
Wisely regardful of th' embroiling sky,
In joyless fields and thorny thickets, leaves
His shivering mates, and pays to
   trusted man
His annual visit. Half afraid, he first
Against the window beats; then,
   brisk, alights
On the warm hearth; then, hopping o'er
   the floor,
Eyes all the smiling family askance,
And pecks, and starts, and wonders where
   he is;
Till, more familiar grown, the table crumbs
Attract his slender feet.

JAMES THOMSON

February

17

18

19

20

February

... THE DIM CLOUD *that does the
world enfold*
Hath less the characters of dark and cold
Than warmth and light asleep,
And correspondent breathing seems to keep
*With the infant harvest, breathing
  soft below*
Its eider coverlet of snow.
Nor is in field or garden anything
But, duly look'd into, contains serene
*The substance of things hoped for, in
  the spring,*
And evidence of summer not yet seen.

COVENTRY PATMORE

21

22

February

Ere the snowdrop peepeth,
　Ere the crocus bold,
Ere the early primrose
　Opes its paly gold,
Somewhere on a sunny bank
　Buttercups are bright;
Somewhere 'mong the frozen grass
　Peeps the daisy white.

MARY HOWITT

23

24

25

February

26

28

27

29

March

ROSSLAND DAFFODILS

March

1

Fine March weather: boisterous, blustering, much wind and squalls of rain; and yet the sky, where the clouds are swept away, deliciously blue, with snatches of sunshine, bright, and clear, and healthful, and the roads, in spite of the slight glittering showers, crisply dry. Altogether the day is tempting, very tempting.

MARY RUSSELL MITFORD

2

3

March

4

5

ALL DAY THE *winter seemed to have gone.*

Far off, for the first time in the year, a ploughboy, who remembered spring and knew it would come again, shouted 'Cuckoo! Cuckoo!' A warm wind swept over the humid pastures and red sand-pits on the hills and they gleamed in a light muffled sun. Once more in the valleys the ruddy farmhouses and farm-buildings seemed new and fair again, and the oast-house cones stood up as prophets of spring . . .

The leaves of goosegrass, mustard, vetch, dog's mercury, were high above the dead leaves on hedge banks. Primrose and periwinkle were blossoming . . .

In the elms, sitting crosswise on a bough, sang thrush and missel thrush; in the young corn, the larks, the robins in the thorns; and in all the meadows the guttural notes of the rooks were mellowed by love and the sun.

EDWARD THOMAS

March

6

7

8

9

March

10

11

12

*T*HE WIND BLEW *briskly, and the lake was covered all over with bright silver waves, that were there each the twinkling of an eye, then others rose up and took their place as fast as they went away. The rooks glittered in the sunshine, the crows and the ravens were busy, and the thrushes and little birds sang. I went through the fields, and sat half an hour afraid to pass a Cow. The Cow looked at me, and I looked at the Cow, and whenever I stirred the Cow gave over eating.*

DOROTHY WORDSWORTH

March

13

15

14

16

March

17

18

19

20

March

21

> *Happy, happy earth! Fit habitation for gods, which, so short a time before, was bleak, damp, and unwholesome. My spirits were elevated by the enchanting appearance of nature; the past was blotted from my memory, the present was tranquil, and the future gilded by bright rays of hope and anticipations of joy.*
>
> MARY SHELLEY

22

23

March

24

25

26

27

March

28

30

29

31

April

OPPOSITE WINDOWS

April

1

2

APRIL 20 (1874) *This has been a very beautiful day – fields about us deep green lighted underneath with white daisies, yellower fresh green of leaves above which bathes the skirts of the elms, and their tops are touched and worded with leaf too. Looked at the big limb of that elm that hangs over into the park and the swinggate further out than where the leaves were open and saw beautiful inscape, home-coiling wiry bushes of spray, touched with bud to point them. Blue shadows fell all up the meadow at sunset and then standing at the far park corner my eye was struck by such a sense of green in the tufts and pashes of grass, with purple shadow thrown back on the dry black mould behind them, as I do not remember ever to have been exceeded in looking at green grass.*

GERARD MANLEY HOPKINS

April

3

4

5

*F*AIR DAFFODILS, *we weep to see*
    You haste away so soon:
As yet the early-rising sun
Has not attain'd his noon.
   Stay, stay
Until the hasting day
   Has run
But to the even-song;
And, having pray'd together, we
Will go with you along.

ROBERT HERRICK

April

6

8

7

9

April

10

11

12

Now fades the last long streak of snow,
   Now burgeons every maze of quick
About the flowering squares, and thick
By ashen roots the violets blow.

Now rings the woodland loud and long,
The distance takes a lovelier hue,
And drowned in yonder living blue
The lark becomes a sightless song.

From land to land; and in my breast
Spring wakens too; and my regret
Becomes an April violet,
And buds and blossoms like the rest.

ALFRED, LORD TENNYSON

April

13

15

14

16

April

Along the blushing borders
   bright with dew,
And in yon mingled wilderness
   of flowers,
Fair handed spring unbosoms every
   grace:
Throws out the snow-drop and the
   crocus first;
The daisy, primrose, violet darkly blue,
And polyanthus of unnumbered dyes;
The yellow wall-flower, stained with
   iron brown,
And lavish stock that scents the
   garden round.

JAMES THOMSON

18

17

19

April

20

21

22

23

April

24

25

26

27

April

28

29

30

> Now, in the last week of April, the cherry blossom is still white, but waning and passing away: it is late this year; and the leaves are clustering thick and softly copper in their dark blood-filled glow. The pear and the peach were out together. But now the pear tree is a lovely thick softness of new and glossy green, vivid with a tender fullness of apple-green leaves, gleaming among all the other green of the landscape. The wheat may shine lit-up yellow, or glow bluish, but the pear tree is green in itself.
>
> D. H. LAWRENCE

May

WINDOW GEESE

May

1

2

3

I HAVE SEEN THE *rosebud blow,*
   And in the jocund sunbeam glow,
Sportive lambs on airy mound,
Skipping o'er the velvet ground;
And the sprightly-footed morn,
When every hedge and every thorn
Was decked in spring's apparel gay,
All the pride of opening May:

MARIA COWPER

May

4

5

6

7

May

WHEN THOMASIN WITHDREW *the curtains, there stood the Maypole. The sweet perfume of the flowers had already spread into the surrounding air. At the top of the pole were crossed hoops decked with small flowers; beneath these came a milk-white zone of Maybloom; then of lilacs, then of ragged robins, daffodils, and soon Thomasin noticed all these, and was delighted that the May-revel was to be so near.*

THOMAS HARDY

9

8

10

May

11

12

13

The young bullfinches in their party coloured raiment bustle about among the blossoms and poise themselves like wire-dancers or tumblers, shaking the twigs and dashing off the blossoms. There is yet one primrose in the orchard. The wild columbines are coming into beauty. In the garden we have lilies and many other flowers. The scarlet beans are up in crowds; May roses blossoming.

DOROTHY WORDSWORTH

May

14

15

16

17

May

A SUNNY SHAFT DID *I behold*,
    From sky to earth it slanted:
And poised therein a bird so bold –
    Sweet bird, thou wert enchanted!
He sank, he rose, he twinkled, he trolled
    Within that shaft of sunny mist;
His eyes of fire, his beak of gold,
    All else of amethyst!

And thus he sang: 'Adieu! adieu!
    Sweet month of May,
        We must away;
           Far, far away!
              To day! to day!'

SAMUEL TAYLOR COLERIDGE

18

19

20

May

21

23

22

24

May

25

27

26

28

May

*W*HEN ALL THE WORLD *is young, lad,*
    And all the trees are green;
And every goose a swan, lad,
    And every lass a queen;
Then hey for boot and horse, lad,
    And round the world away;
Young blood must have its course, lad,
    And every dog his day.

CHARLES KINGSLEY

30

29

31

June

THE LABURNUM CAT

June

1

2

A SPLENDID MIDSUMMER shone over England: skies so pure, suns so radiant as were then seen in long succession, seldom favour, even singly, our wave-girt land. It was as if a band of Italian days had come from the south, like a flock of glorious passenger birds, and lighted to rest them on the cliffs of Albion. The hay was all got in; the fields round Thornfield were green and shorn, the roads white and baked; the trees were in their dark prime; hedge and wood, full-leaved and deeply-tinted, contrasted well with the sunny hue of the cleared meadows between.

It was now the sweetest hour of the twenty-four – 'Day its fervid fires had wasted,' and dew fell cool on panting plain and scorched summit. Where the sun had gone down in simple state – pure of the pomp of the clouds – spread a solemn purple, burning with the light of red jewel and furnace flame at one point, on one hill-peak, and extending high and wide, soft and still softer, over half heaven. The east had its own charm of fine deep blue, and its own modest gem, a rising and solitary star: soon it would boast the moon; but she was yet beneath the horizon.

CHARLOTTE BRONTË

June

3

5

4

6

June

7

*I*N WINTER I GET *up at night*
  And dress by yellow candle-light.
In summer, quite the other way,
I have to go to bed by day.

I have to go to bed and see
The birds still hopping on the tree,
Or hear the grown-up people's feet
Still going past me in the street.

And does it not seem hard to you,
When all the sky is clear and blue,
And I should like so much to play,
To have to go to bed by day?

ROBERT LOUIS STEVENSON

8

9

June

10

11

12

*T*HE GARLANDS FADE *that Spring so
    lately wove,*
*Each simple flower, which she had
    nursed in dew,*
*Anemonies, that spangled every grove,
    The primrose wan, and harebell
    mildly blue.*
*No more shall violets linger in the dell,
    Or purple orchis variegate the plain,*
*Till Spring again shall call forth every bell,
    And dress with humid hands her
    wreaths again. –*

CHARLOTTE SMITH

June

13

15

14

16

June

17

The season developed and matured. Another year's instalment of flowers, leaves, nightingales, thrushes, finches, and such ephemeral creatures, took up their positions where only a year ago others had stood in their place when these were nothing more than germs and inorganic particles. Rays from the sunrise drew forth the buds and stretched them into long stalks, lifted up sap in noiseless streams, opened petals, and sucked out scents in invisible jets and breathings...

THOMAS HARDY

18

19

June

20

21

22

23

June

24

25

26

27

June

28

29

30

To awake as the summer sun came slanting over hill-tops, with hope on every beam a-dance to the laughter of the morning; to see the leaves across the window ruffling on the fresh new air, and the tendrils of the powdery vine turning from their beaded sleep. Then the lustrous meadows far beyond the thatch of the garden wall, yet seen beneath the hanging scollops of the walnut tree, all awaking, dressed in pearl, all amazed at their own glistening, like a maid at her own ideas.

R. D. BLACKMORE

July

BOEF VAN KEULEN

July

1

2

3

He said the pleasantest manner of spending a hot July day was lying from morning till evening on a bank of heath in the middle of the moors, with the bees humming dreamily about among the bloom, and the larks singing high up over head, and the blue sky and bright sun shining steadily and cloudlessly. That was his most perfect idea of heaven's happiness.

EMILY BRONTË

July

4

6

5

7

July

Oh! how some of those idle fellows longed to be outside, and how they looked at the open door and window.

What rebellious thoughts of the cool river, and some shady bathing-place, kept tempting and urging that sturdy boy, who, with his shirt collar unbuttoned and flung back as far as it could go, sat fanning his flushed face with a spelling-book, wishing himself a whale, or a tittlebat, or a fly, or anything but a boy at school on that hot, broiling day!

CHARLES DICKENS

8

9

10

July

11

13

12

*How sweet it were, hearing the
downward stream,
With half-shut eyes ever to seem
Falling asleep in a half-dream!
To dream and dream, like yonder
   amber light,
Which will not leave the myrrh-
   bush on the height;
To hear each other's whispered
   speech;
Eating the Lotos day by day,
To watch the crisping ripples on
   the beach,
And tender curving lines of creamy
   spray . . .*

ALFRED, LORD TENNYSON

July

14

16

15

17

July

*I LOVE AT EVENTIDE to walk alone
Down narrow lanes o'erhung
with dewy thorn
Where from the long grass
underneath the snail
Jet black creeps out and sprouts his
timid horn
I love to muse o'er meadows newly
mown
Where withering grass perfumes the
sultry air
Where bees search round with sad and
weary drone
In vain for flowers that bloomed but
newly there.*

JOHN CLARE

18

19

20

July

21

23

22

24

July

25

27

26

28

July

29

30

31

There was much most beautiful in the fresh level meadows on each side of the road. A group of cattle, very young and very gentle, lying on a little promontory of cool grass in the shade, and yet so brown and bright white that they looked like sunshine, and lay as quietly, the water-lilies resting like them in their own place – their bud-like poppy-seed fruit, poised in the deep water – and a fair, far reaching sky, all full of white clouds like endless marble stairs.

JOHN RUSKIN

August

AUSTRIAN PEARS

August

*T*HE FIELDS ARE ALL *alive with busy noise*
   Of labours sounds and insects
  humming joys
Some o'er the glittering sickle sweating stoop
Startling full oft the partridge coveys up
Some o'er the rustling scythe go bending on
And shockers follow where their toils
  have gone
First turning swaths to wither in the sun
Where mice from terrors dangers nimbly run

JOHN CLARE

1

2

3

August

4

5

6

*T*HE SEA WAS LIKE *blue silk. It seemed warped over towards our feet. Half-miles of catspaw like breathing on glass just turned the smoothness here and there. Red cliffs, white ashy shingle, green inshore water, blue above that, clouds and distant cliffs dropping soft white beams down it, bigger clouds making big white tufts broken by ripples of the darker blue foreground water as if they were great white roses sunk in a blue dye.*

GERARD MANLEY HOPKINS

August

7

9

8

10

August

11

13

12

14

August

15

16

17

We have lived a few days on the seashore, with the waves banging up at us: with pale sand, and very much white foam, row after row, coming from under the sky, in the silver evening. It is a great thing to realise that the original world is still there — perfectly clean and pure, many white advancing foams, and only the gulls swinging between the sky and the shore.

D. H. LAWRENCE

August

18

19

20

21

August

22

23

24

In summer when the woods are green
  And leaves are large and long,
Full merry it is in the fair forest
  To hear the small birds' song.

To see the red deer seek the dale
  And leave the hills so high,
To shade themselves among the glades
  Under the greenwood tree.

OLD BALLAD

August

25

26

27

28

August

29

30

31

> Thursday, the thirty-first of August, was one of a series of days during which snug houses were stifling, and when cool draughts were treats; when cracks appeared in clayey gardens, and were called 'earthquakes' by apprehensive children; and when stinging insects haunted the air, the earth and every drop of water that was to be found.
>
> THOMAS HARDY

September

FIVE GREEN APPLES

September

1

2

*T*ELL ME NOT HERE, *it needs not saying,*
   What tune the enchantress plays
In aftermaths of soft September
Or under blanching mays,
She and I were long acquainted
And I knew all her ways.

On russet floors, by waters idle,
The pine lets fall its cone;
The cuckoo shouts all day at nothing
In leafy dells alone;
And traveller's joy beguiles in autumn
Hearts that have lost their own.

On acres of the seeded grasses
The changing burnish leaves;
Or marshalled under moons of harvest
Stand still all night the sheaves;
Or beeches strip in storms for winter
And stain the wind with leaves.

A. E. HOUSMAN

September

3

5

4

6

September

Welcome to you, rich Autumn days,
　Ere comes the cold, leaf-picking
　　　wind;
When golden stocks are seen in fields,
All standing arm-in-arm entwined;
　And gallons of sweet cider seen
　On trees in apples red and green.

With mellow pears that cheat our teeth,
Which melt that tongues may suck
　them in;
With blue-black damsons, yellow plums,
　And woodnuts rich, to make us go
　Into the loneliest lanes we know.

W. H. DAVIES

7

8

9

September

10

11

12

A day of exceeding and almost unmatched beauty ... A warm delicious calm and sweet peace brooded breathless over the mellow sunny autumn afternoon and the happy stillness was broken only by the voices of children blackberry gathering in an adjoining meadow and the occasional pattering of an acorn or a chestnut through the leaves to the ground.

FRANCIS KILVERT

September

13

15

14

16

September

Goodbye, goodbye to summer!
  For summer's nearly done;
The garden smiling faintly,
  Cool breezes in the sun;
Our thrushes now are silent,
  Our swallows flown away—
But Robin's here, in coat of brown,
  With ruddy breast-knot gay.
Robin, Robin Redbreast,
  O Robin dear!
Robin singing sweetly
  In the falling of the year.

WILLIAM ALLINGHAM

17

18

19

September

20

22

21

23

September

24

26

25

27

September

28

29

30

*C*OME, LOVE, FOR NOW *the night and day*
  Play with their pawns of black
    and white,
And what day loses in her play
  Is won by the encroaching night.

The clematis grows old and clings
  Grey-bearded to the road-side trees
And in the hedge the nightshade strings
  Her berries in bright necklaces.

The fields are bare; the latest sheaf
  Of barley, wheat and rusty rye
Is stacked long since; and every leaf
  Burns like a sunset on the sky.

A. J. YOUNG

October

ROASTING ON THE RADIATOR

October

The late year has grown fresh again and new
As spring, and to the touch is not more
* cool*
Than it is warm to the gaze; and now
* I might*
As happy be as earth is beautiful.

EDWARD THOMAS

1

2

3

October

4

6

5

7

October

O, THE SWEET MELANCHOLY of the time
   When gently, ere the heart
  appeals, the year
Shines in the fatal beauty of decay!
When the sun sinks enlarged on
   Carronben,
Nakedly visible, without a cloud,
And faintly from the faint eternal blue . . .
Comes the star which evening wears
And in the cottage windows, one by one,
With sudden twinkle household lamps
   are lit –
What noiseless falling of the faded leaf!

DAVID GRAY

8

9

10

October

11

12

13

*See the kitten on the wall,
     Sporting with the leaves that fall,
Withered leaves, one, two and three,
Falling from the elder-tree;
Through the calm and frosty air
Of the morning bright and fair.*

*See the kitten, how she starts,
Crouches, stretches, paws and darts;
With a tiger-leap half way
Now she meets her coming prey.
Lets it go as fast as then
Has it in her power again.*

WILLIAM WORDSWORTH

October

14

15

16

17

October

18

19

20

21

October

22

*I've seen the smiling of Fortune beguiling,
I've felt all its favours and found its decay;
I've seen the Forest adorned the foremost,
With flowers of the fairest, most pleasant and gay;
Sae bonny was their blooming, their scents the air perfuming;
But now they are withered and wade all away*

ALISON COCKBURN

23

24

October

25

27

26

28

October

29

30

31

At the end of the month hard frosts. Wonderful downpour of leaf: when the morning sun began to melt the frost they fell at one touch and in a few minutes a whole tree was flung of them; they lay masking and papering the ground at the foot.

GERARD MANLEY HOPKINS

November

ST. HELIER DORMER CAT

November

1

2

3

Summer fading, *winter comes —*
Frosty mornings, tingling thumbs,
Window robins, winter rooks,
And the picture story-books.

Water now is turned to stone
Nurse and I can walk upon;
Still we find the flowing brooks
In the picture story-books.

ROBERT LOUIS STEVENSON

November

4

5

6

7

November

9

It was a rimy morning, and very damp. I had seen the damp lying on the outside of my little window, as if some goblin had been crying there all night, and using the window for a pocket-handkerchief. On every rail and gate, wet lay clammy; and the marsh-mist was so thick, that ... instead of my running at everything, everything seemed to run at me.

CHARLES DICKENS

8

10

November

11

12

13

14

November

15

16

17

What way does the *Wind* come?
What way does he go?
He rides over the water, and over the
snow,
Through wood, and through vale;
and o'er rocky height,
Which the goat cannot climb, takes his
sounding flight . . .

Yet seek him – and what shall you
find in his place?
Nothing but silence and empty space;
Save, in a corner, a heap of dry leaves,
That he's left, for a bed, to beggars or
thieves!

DOROTHY WORDSWORTH

November

18

19

20

21

November

22

> *R*ED SUNS AND TUFTS *of fire one by one began to arise, flecking the whole country round. They were the bonfires of other parishes and hamlets that were engaged in the same sort of commemoration.*
>
> *The first tall flame from Rainbarrow sprang into the sky.*
>
> *The cheerful blaze streaked the inner surface of the human circle with its own gold livery, and even overlaid the dark turf around with a lively luminousness.*
>
> THOMAS HARDY

23

24

November

25

26

There had not been such a winter for years. It came on in stealthy and measured glides, like the moves of a chess-player. Every twig was covered with a white nap as of fur grown from the rind during the night, giving it four times its usual stoutness; the whole bush or tree forming a staring sketch in white lines on the mournful gray of the sky and horizon. Cobwebs revealed their presence on shed and walls where none had ever been observed till brought out into visibility by the crystallizing atmosphere, hanging like loops of white worsted from salient points of the out-houses, posts, and gates.

THOMAS HARDY

November

27

28

29

30

December

THE CHRISTMAS GOOSE

December

1

2

*B*OB SAID HE DIDN'T *believe there ever was such a goose cooked. Its tenderness and flavour, size and cheapness were the themes of universal admiration. Eked out by apple sauce and mashed potatoes, it was sufficient dinner for the whole family... everyone had had enough and the youngest Cratchits in particular were steeped in sage and onion to the eyebrows... In half a minute Mrs Cratchit entered flushed, but smiling proudly – with the pudding, like a speckled cannon-ball, so hard and firm, blazing in half of half-a-quartern of ignited brandy, and bedight with Christmas holly stuck on the top.*

CHARLES DICKENS

December

3

4

5

6

December

*G*LAD CHRISTMAS COMES, *and every hearth*
  Makes room to give him welcome now,
E'en want will dry its tears in mirth,
  And crown him with a holly bough;

Each house is swept the day before,
  And windows stuck with evergreens,
The snow is besom'd from the door,
  And comfort crowns the cottage scenes.

JOHN CLARE

8

7

9

December

10

11

12

13

December

14

15

16

17

December

18

19

20

The blue mountains were silver ribbed with snow and looked like a dead giant lying in state – a Titan ... home by the upper road crazy with face ache, weak and wretched, and the road never seemed to be so long. After dinner and four glasses of port I felt better.

FRANCIS KILVERT

December

21

23

22

24

December

25

27

26

28

December

29

30

31

Late lies the wintry sun a-bed,
A frosty, fiery sleepy-head;
Blinks but an hour or two; and then,
A blood-red orange, sets again.

Before the stars have left the skies,
At morning in the dark I rise;
And shivering in my nakedness,
By the cold candle, bathe and dress.

Close by the jolly fire I sit
To warm my frozen bones a bit;
Or with a reindeer-sled, explore
The colder countries round the door.

ROBERT LOUIS STEVENSON